MW00785101

SAUDI ARABIA: THE IMPRESSIVE TRUTH

EXPERIENCING THE VALUES AND GOODNESS INSIDE THE KINGDOM

Michael F Andrew

The Empire Publishers publishing

131 Finsbury Pavement, London EC2A 1NT

https://www.theempirepublishers.co.uk/

Our books may be purchased in bulk for promotional, educational, or business use.

Please contact The Empire Publishers at +44 20 4579 8116, or by email at support@theempirepublishers.co.uk

First Edition July 2024

"The most complete of the believers in faith, is the one with the best character among them."

Hadith from Prophet Muhammed (PBUH)

"Thou shalt love the Lord thy God with all thy heart, and with all they soul and with all your mind"

Jesus according to Matthew 22:37-40

"I believe that the only true religion consists of having a good heart"

Dalai Lama

About the Author

Michael was born and raised in the suburbs of Boston, Massachusetts, in the United States. He has held numerous executive roles and was a board advisor, board member, leadership author, leadership consultant, and executive coach. As of this writing, he is an "Advisor" for a multi-billion-dollar company in Saudi Arabia. He owned a global consulting practice and is the author of three other books. The first, "How to Think Like a CEO and Act Like a Leader," offers practical insights on business acumen and leadership and was featured on Fox Morning News in Boston. The second book, "The Greatest Leader He Ever Saw," focuses on leadership with a foundation of integrity, humility, and treating people with dignity. Finally, a fiction book entitled, "LUKE: a boy's inspiring journey of lessons learned through setbacks, triumphs, humility, and love." Mike has lived the past ten years (as of this writing) in Saudi Arabia and five years before that in Dubai. He has traveled to many parts of the world for his work.

He earned a Bachelor's Degree in Business, an MBA, and a post-MBA Certificate in Advanced Management Studies.

You can view Mike's leadership videos, as well as videos delivering his views about the Middle East and Saudi Arabia, on his social media channels:

LinkedIn: @mikeandrew11

YouTube: @mfandrew

TikTok: @mfandrew11

Dedication

With a profound love and pride for my one and only child, my dear son, Michael Todd, a special needs child who is a true blessing in my life and demonstrates every day the goodness of a pure and innocent heart, I have experienced a father's unwavering and protective love and devotion.

I am grateful to all my dear friends and colleagues from the Kingdom of Saudi Arabia. Thank you for welcoming me into your homes, accepting me as a friend and colleague, and offering me the professional opportunities of a lifetime. This is what inspired me to write this book in order to share the goodness, goodwill, and values of the Saudi people.

Finally, I honor the loving memory of my beloved parents, George and Gertrude, and my dear younger brother, Todd.

Acknowledgments

I offer my deep appreciation to those who contributed to this book by offering insightful feedback, ideas, ensuring accuracy, and providing strong encouragement: Ibrahim M. Balghonaim (Abu Mosab), Faiez Awadh (Abu Mohamed), Ghaida S. Al-Qahtani (Umm Aljohara), Saud Alsherhaihi (Abu AlBandari), Mohammed A. Alabbadi (Abu Abdullah), Mathad F. Alajmi (Abu Faisal), Dr. Shaker H. Almahasna (Abu Maryam), Abdullah A. Alkanhal (Abu Abdulrahman), Fahd Alghamdi (Abu Abdulaziz), Bader A. Abdulqader (Abu Faisal), Abdulaziz M. Alhaider (Abu Haya), Dr. Moudhi M. Aljamea, Wijnand Van Till (Abu Florijn), Refan Althumairy, Abdulaziz B. Bawazeer (Abu Abdullah), Ahmad M.S. Alghamdi (Abu Waleed), Hani W. Alahdal (Abu Khalid),Khalid M. Aljarboa (Abu Mohammed), Ivan Koncharov (Abu Dariy), Bassam A. Alsuwayyigh (Abu Abdullah),

Khulud Barnawi, Jamal Shah (Abu Jilal), Chris Lamatsch (Abu Kay), Rory Hendrikz (Abu Zara), and Norah A. Alomair.

I am grateful for the friendship and acts of kindness from hundreds of my dear colleagues. Each of you (and you know who you are) has made my final working years the most rewarding. Shukran Jazeelan (Thank you).

I have always maintained that a capable editor makes any writer look good. The same goes to Ms. Dianne Williams, from The Empire Publishers who has impressed me with her work and made this book a better read. I thank Ms. Phoebe Collins as well who managed the publication process. I was certainly in good hands with you both.

TABLE OF CONTENTS

Introduction

The purpose of this short book is to share my experiences as an American executive living and working in the Middle East. I spent five years in Dubai and Abu Dhabi in the United Arab Emirates and ten years (still ongoing as of this writing) in the Kingdom of Saudi Arabia. Quite simply, this experience has enhanced my life.

Living and working in the Middle East and interacting with so many Saudi citizens and some Emirati citizens have transformed and shattered my lifelong perceptions. The negative perceptions of places like Saudi Arabia are deeply ingrained in a large percentage of Americans and Westerners. Perceptions such as how women are treated and the intolerance toward other religions and cultures have been completely diminished by my experiences, which you will see, and hopefully, understand.

I often find it a difficult challenge when I try to discuss a different view with my fellow Americans. The good news is that many listen with an open mind and take genuine interest in my views and are surprised to hear what I have to share. That is where tolerance begins—by seeking first to understand. I've always said that if I had not lived in the Middle East for all these years, my views would undoubtedly be consistent with everyone else's, primarily as conveyed and portrayed by the media. As a result, it can be difficult for one to be open to a different view. I hope my firsthand experiences presented in this book will open the reader's mind. I feel this is important, as we can all learn from different cultures around the world, including the people from Saudi Arabia and other Middle Eastern countries. The teachings and practices of Muslims, from what I see every day, emphasize that since we are all created by one God, we must treat one another with dignity, respect, and kindness.

The beginning of this book conveys my early career in the United States. I then offer stories about living and working in the United Arab Emirates, mainly in Dubai and Abu Dhabi, which began my introduction to Middle Eastern culture. But the most profound and meaningful stories will come from my life in Saudi Arabia.

I hope the following stories, with lessons learned and examples of how kind humanity can be, will resonate with you, the reader. Every single day I am grateful for experiencing the kindness and respect demonstrated to me. I have learned and experienced the notion of truly feeling welcomed. Living in Saudi Arabia has completely revamped the preconceived notions that had littered my mind before and has been the antithesis of my original expectations of what I was convinced I was going to experience.

Let me end this introduction with this comment: Living in Saudi Arabia, Dubai, and Abu Dhabi has changed my life – all in the best ways possible. It is not about the landscape. To me, there is nothing more beautiful than the New England landscape with its mountains, lakes, and ocean where I grew up. It is about the decency, kindness, hospitality, and humanity of the people in the Middle East, most notably the people from Saudi Arabia. These attributes are based on their foundational beliefs, teachings, and values. Pure and simply, they are based on the foundation of God (Allah) in their lives.

To the reader, please keep an open mind. There is much we can learn from each other's experiences and from other cultures around the world. I hope you enjoy these stories, as they represent just a very small portion of what I have experienced and learned.

Michael F Andrew

Riyadh, Kingdom of Saudi Arabia

Laconia, NH, United States of America

PART 1: EARLY CAREER YEARS IN THE USA

The United States did many good things for me. It gave me a wonderful childhood with many athletic memories, which instilled in me a certain level of confidence I needed as a young man. By attaining certain skills and achievements in sports, I had no choice but to learn about humility from failures that derive from not always winning and sometimes playing poorly. The United States also provided me with a great foundation in my education and early career. In later years, it disappointed me. It was all for the better. Though I am proud of my achievements, I am also grateful for the pain and setbacks. It is a common story we all experience, and they provide great lessons in life. It is about persevering and how things almost always end up working out for the best.

My story starts with growing up in the Boston area and eventually taking on corporate roles in the Chicago and Milwaukee areas. Lifelong memories and lessons were created for sure as I moved further in my personal and professional journey.

I was very fortunate in that I had one company pay for my MBA (as long as I maintained a 3.0 or "B" average, which you must attain in order to graduate with an MBA) and another company paid for my post-MBA studies. Achieving an MBA was one of my first career goals. As my Italian grandmother, Erminia ("Minnie") Simonelli Cianciulli, used to say to me, "No one can take away your education."

Other than that, my career was a typical uphill battle, as it is for most young professionals. I don't believe all career professionals and people working for a living will ever experience a smooth, straight upward path. I wish it were that easy. I describe it like investing in the stock market over the long term. A typical career has its ups and downs, plenty of disappointments, frustrations, setbacks, and closed doors. But it then offers new and often better doors and opportunities. In the end, like a stock investment, your career over time will have achieved that upward climb if you persevere and work hard. I like to say that "things always work out for the best," even when it is difficult to feel that way at times. As the words in the famous Garth Brooks song say, "I thank God for unanswered prayers." In the song, the person prayed hard for something to happen. It did not happen. That unanswered prayer was devastating for that person. But God had a better plan, and in the end, things worked out far better, and so he "thanked God for that unanswered prayer." The Muslim saying for this concept is "Khairah" – that God knows what is better for us and that things will work out for the best under His guidance.

In my early career journey, I worked hard and hoped harder. I had many hurdles come my way, just as we all do, but I did my best to keep moving forward with both work and graduate school. It took a number of years to finally land a job after graduating college. It was a finance role where everyone around me majored in accounting or finance. It was not the perfect fit, and it certainly was not my strength as I did not major in finance or accounting. But it was a job. Ultimately, this served me extremely well in my later years as I eventually taught "Finance for Non-Financial Managers" and applied my financial acumen coaching managers, executives, and board directors around understanding and interpreting financial statements. Things work out for the best eventually – Khairah.

I think I did all the right things by educating myself, working hard, and focusing on career goals. I worked my way up the corporate ladder to middle-to-senior level roles. But then I stepped out, took a chance, and started a global consulting business. I wrote a book, which was featured on Fox Morning News in Boston. It sold pretty well, and I got some encouraging messages from some well-known people who read and liked the book. The first five years of my consulting business exceeded my best-case scenario in terms of income, lifestyle, and world travel with Fortune 100 companies and consulting firms like McKinsey and Arthur D. Little. It was my business that opened the opportunity to work in the Middle East, starting with a client in Dubai and Abu Dhabi. It was an amazing eye-opener filled with life experiences and lessons learned, which would eventually be life-changing and the inspiration for this book.

I have many good memories of my global travels when I operated my consulting business: the verdant beauty of Scotland, the quaint and bucolic village of Kitzbuhel, Austria, the enjoyment of Sentosa Island in Singapore, the early stages of

Dubai and Abu Dhabi, and of course, throughout the United States. I have many stories, but allow me to share this one with you:

I had a two-week assignment in Milan, Italy. Since I am half Italian, I was pretty excited about this trip. While in Milan, a close and dear lifelong friend, who was the head of a well-known U.S. government agency, suggested I go to Rome during the weekend as he could arrange a private tour of the Vatican. Because of my friend's role, he worked closely with the Pope's private security. In fact, he had met two Popes—Pope John Paul II and Pope Benedict XVI. Arrangements were made for me to go to the Vatican on the weekend and meet the Swiss Guards. One of Pope Benedict's well-dressed protective agents was waiting for me beside a luxury vehicle. We drove around the back of the Vatican where the Pope took his daily walk. I saw the replica of the grotto of Lourdes, France. Lourdes is where the Virgin Mary is said to have appeared to a young

French girl named Bernadette Soubirous in 1858. It was at the replica of the grotto where the Pope stopped to pray daily. I saw the Pope's private train and helicopter and even the burial ground of many deceased Popes. I saw where Pope John Paul II was buried, and I even saw the glass casket of Pope John XXIII, often referred to as the "Good Pope" and the Pope I remember as a young boy. There he was, in his papal clothing and in clear view. Somehow, they preserved his body. I remember feeling every pore of my body drowning in awe of what I was able to see with my eyes during that visit.

As we were driving, I asked the Italian agent, "Do you give private tours like this often?" With his Italian accent, he said, "No, not much. The last time I did this was with Sylvester Stallone." The memory still brings me a good chuckle.

As my business was exceeding my expectations, the 9/11 attacks in New York City and Washington, DC happened. One of the worst recessions in USA history followed shortly after. I went from living the dream to living my worst nightmare. It was devastating and embarrassing. A few years later, I had to declare bankruptcy, losing all my money and having my beautiful home on the lake in New Hampshire repossessed by the bank. Starting a business is always a risk. With risk can come great rewards or great loss. I experienced both. I am grateful for experiencing both – the bliss of my achievements and the severe wrath of my failures. Managing and persevering through the most tumultuous and humiliating times is something I look back on now with pride.

After 10 years of running my own consulting business and in my early 50s, I was not able to get an interview from any company, despite my substantial experience, education, and achievements. I believe age, affirmative action goals, and diversity strategies played a factor, though every company in the United States claims they do not discriminate based on age and race.

I was bankrupt and barely surviving when I received an unexpected, out-of-the-blue call from a former client. They wanted to talk to me about a corporate management role. They flew me to Abu Dhabi. I had no credit card to use as a deposit at the hotel due to my bankruptcy, but the hotel allowed me to check in as the company was one of the largest and most respected in the region.

The following morning, I was driven to the company headquarters where I met with a team of executives. They described the recent restructuring and pointed out a role they wanted me to consider. It was not an interview; it was just a discussion about the restructuring and my interest in the role. I joked with them that they could have done this over the phone. They replied, "We haven't seen you in a while, Mike, so we wanted to see you." I went from being completely broke with no funds to survive, to eventually becoming a Vice President of a multi-billion-dollar company.

When I say the Middle East saved me, I say it with every ounce of my being. They did not care about my age (55 years old at that time) or that I did not fit the DEI (Diversity, Equity, Inclusion) profile. They only cared about my ability to do the job and valued the relationship built over the years. I continue to thank God for unanswered prayers – Khairah.

When I arrived in Dubai in November 2009 to begin my new job, I believed I would last six months because I was still aggressively seeking employment back in the USA. The USA was my home, and that is where I wanted to be. Every week, I applied to an average of 10 jobs in the USA over the course of 6 years and 52 weeks per year. Doing the math, that equals over 3,000 jobs I applied for back in my home country. How many responses did I receive? Zero. Not one phone call, not one interview. Despite this, I kept moving forward and persevering. I remained grateful for my new executive role, which eventually led to a Vice President position, meeting good people, and enjoying life in Dubai. I had good reasons to feel blessed and to keep moving forward. I have no doubt things were meant to be this way. I began to realize that God has our life journey planned out. So, yes, the Middle East not only saved me, it gave me a new life.

PART 2: UNITED ARAB EMIRATES

My Introduction to the Middle East

(2009–2014)

I am sure the reader has heard all the amazing things about Dubai, one of the seven Emirates in the United Arab Emirates. It has the biggest everything: the biggest malls, the tallest building in the world, incredible resorts, a 7-star hotel, amazing and innovative architecture, and much more. I will not get into that here. I will say that I first visited Dubai and Abu Dhabi in January 1996 on behalf of a major global consulting firm. When I returned in 2009 to work full-time, I was shocked at the dramatic and tremendous change and growth. I barely recognized the Dubai I was introduced to. Dubai had turned into a major global city and international financial center. I wish I could tell many more stories, but for the purposes of this book, I will keep it short.

Dubai is mostly populated by citizens from other countries. With most of the population being non-Emiratis and as it is now an international city and tourist destination, Dubai does not have the pure Middle Eastern feel, though there is enough of the Arab culture consisting of the wonderful kindness and hospitality of the Emirati people.

I learned many valuable lessons while living in the United Arab Emirates. I had an office in both Dubai and Abu Dhabi. Building trust by managing the relationship with my boss was a key lesson. I was first hired in a role reporting to a talented Emirati woman who was the youngest Vice President in the company's history, as well as the first female Vice President in the company's history. She was on an accelerated executive track. The company was one of the most established in the United Arab Emirates and the Gulf region. It was a well-known and well-respected brand. Her role as a VP stressed her out as she seemed to struggle. At first, I was bitter and complained because I was not allowed to do the many things I wanted to do and what I was hired to do. She was very risk-averse and too careful. Nothing was really being accomplished. I realized that my complaining and bitterness were not going to get me anywhere. So, one day I walked into her office. I told her I am here to help her and the team and I wanted to see her succeed. That simple effort opened up the relationship. Trust began to be established. She confided in me about many issues. One day, a few months later, she called me into her office. She handed me a confidential memo and stated, "Mike, I want to share this with you, and you are the first to see this." It was her resignation letter.

I was somewhat stunned but quickly realized I should not be surprised as she seemed to be struggling. Her next comment was, "and I am recommending you to be the next Vice President."

All managers, even the most senior level of executives, need all the help they can get. I believe we all have an unwritten responsibility to manage the relationship with our manager. They don't teach this in business school or in leadership training. Your boss is arguably your most important stakeholder at work. This applies whether you are a CEO reporting to the Chairman of the Board, a VP reporting to a CEO, or an entry-level professional reporting to a manager. Step up and find ways to help them. There is a saying, "Keep your boss's boss off your boss's back."

Before I became a Vice President, I was almost fired. I was asked to work with the CEO and put together a personalized, individual development process to enhance his leadership and general business acumen. It was to be a private, one-on-one, personal tutoring-type of training from business school professors, consulting firms, etc. So, I went to work determining the priority development areas for this CEO. I started contacting my network from business schools and consulting firms. It turns out that our company was populated by some of the top consulting firms (McKinsey, Boston Consulting Group, and others). I spoke to one of the partners in the European office at one of these firms whom I knew quite well. I outlined the requirements and the scope and what area of personalized expertise and tutoring his firm could provide. I never mentioned it was for the CEO. Yet, this consultant seemed to assume it was the CEO. He subsequently mentioned this to the partner on site at our company. This consulting partner saw the CEO on the elevator and mentioned to him that they are in the process of providing a proposal to coach and tutor him. The CEO was embarrassed and enraged. He screamed at my top boss, who, in turn, was screaming about me and basically calling for my head. Fortunately, and with the truth behind me, I never told any of the prospective business schools or consulting firms this was for the CEO (and, by the way, there actually should be nothing wrong with that). As he called me into his office, I went on the offensive and pointed my finger and became quite aggressive with him, basically saying, "how dare you make that assumption about me!" He never expected my reaction and depth of my truthful conviction of being blamed for something that did not happen. In the end, he apologized, shook hands, and I continued to have a job. My current boss at that time (the female Vice President) was in the office during this blowout, and she later told me she never saw anyone address our big boss that assertively and firmly. One month later, I was appointed Vice President.

"Abu" and "Umm:" One of the beautiful things I admire in Arab culture is that every father, aside from his name, also has an "Abu" name, and every mother has an "Umm" name. Abu means "father of" and Umm means "mother of." The Abu or Umm is usually the name of the first son or oldest child. Since my only child is a son named Michael, they often refer to me as "Abu Michael" or "Abu Mike,"

which always brings a smile to my face and a feeling of pride. Imagine trying to remember two names for each person! I see that most people are referred to at work by their Abu name. They use Abu and Umm as a sign of respect to the other person rather than calling him or her by their first name. This also applies whether they are a prince, sheikh, CEO, etc. If you notice in the "Acknowledgments" at the beginning of this book, I refer to each person who supported me with their Abu and Umm names along with their real names.

"Inshallah:" A very common expression in the Middle East is the Arabic phrase "Inshallah." It means "if God wills." For example, if you make plans with someone, you may say, "I will see you tomorrow," and they may respond, "Inshallah." It does not mean "maybe." It is with the understanding and belief that everything in life is in God's hands.

What's So Funny About a Car Accident? One of my colleagues, Faisal, who was a Vice President in our company and a good friend, got me a good deal on a car lease. On my first day driving from Dubai to my main office in Abu Dhabi, just a few minutes from the office, I decided to respond to an email on my phone. A bad mistake. As a result of typing an email response, I collided with the car in front of me. My fault all the way. The driver of the other car was a military General. He was a true gentleman. My biggest worry was how I was going to explain this to my friend Faisal, who went out of his way to get me a good deal on this lease. I walked to his office, and he seemed to have interpreted the look on my face and asked, "Did you get in an accident?" I said yes, and Faisal, being Faisal, burst out laughing and immediately called the President of the leasing company. They were speaking in Arabic and laughing hysterically! I realized that there was no need to be upset any further. The leasing company replaced the car that day (my car had lots of damage). It reminds me of the lesson from Oscar Wilde that "life is too important to be taken seriously."

The Oldest Son of Former Egyptian President Anwar Sadat: In my capacity with my company in the UAE, I was required to visit our Egyptian subsidiary. I was in a meeting with one of the most humble men I have ever met—the oldest son of Anwar El-Sadat, the former President of Egypt from 1970–1981. His name is Gamal. Gamal was the Chairman of our Egyptian company and such a very impressive and decent man. He demonstrated an inimitable executive presence. I remember meeting with him during a break and talking about his father, the former President, and the impact his father's death had on the American public and me personally. It was an honor for me to meet a person with such humility.

Cairo, Egypt: The efforts our company in Egypt made to make me feel welcomed were second to none. When I landed in Cairo, I was walking down the steps of the plane onto the tarmac to take a shuttle bus with the other passengers to the terminal to go through immigration. As I walked down the steps, there was a shiny black Mercedes-Benz with a driver standing in front of the car waiting for a passenger. I thought to myself, "There must be a dignitary on board." At the bottom of the steps before entering the bus, I looked at the driver who was holding a sign. It had my name on it. A definite surprise for sure. He drove me to the terminal, where they escorted me to a private lounge with comfortable sofas and prepared me some coffee. Someone there took my passport and told me to be comfortable while he processed my immigration entry. From there, they drove me in another luxury vehicle to the hotel, where the General Manager of the hotel was waiting outside to greet me. He checked me in and then personally escorted me to my room with a view overlooking the Nile River. It was the first, only time, and I am sure the last time I was made to feel extra special. I share this story as it is a fond memory.

Watching Out For My Safety: I have to give my former company credit. We had a Risk and Crisis Management department that looked not only at business risks and mitigation plans for major strategic initiatives related to our strategy but also at the traveling risks of those traveling on business. If a dangerous situation occurred while traveling, they had a crisis management team ready to act. Since we conducted business in some countries deemed to be risky, it was common to have proactive plans in place in the event a company representative experienced potential danger while traveling on business. I was in Cairo during another trip when we found out that there was going to be a planned "Arab Spring" uprising. My company cut my trip short and ordered me to fly back the following day. They adjusted my ticket, and I arrived back in Dubai without any problems. I am grateful to this day.

Turning Down an Offer of a Lifetime and the Unexpected Twists and "Khairah" That Resulted: During my fifth year in the United Arab Emirates, I was unexpectedly handed the job of a lifetime. It was not a job I applied for, yet it was a job I dreamed of, a job that was aligned with my career ambitions. I was offered a very lucrative role with AT&T in Dallas, Texas. It was going to provide me with three bonus plans, large yearly "grants" of stock, and a spot on the succession plan. This would have been the perfect capstone of my corporate career. This was why I completed my MBA and other post-graduate studies. I worked hard all my life for this moment. And it would have brought me back to the USA. I went so far as to take the drug test. For two weeks, I could not make my final decision. It should have been a no-brainer. I was angry and disappointed at myself for being so indecisive. Something extremely powerful pulled inside me, far more than a gut feeling. I truly believe to this day it was Divine intervention. It was the first and only time I experienced something so powerfully visceral. It was such a profound feeling, a strong intuition, or pull, that I had never experienced and probably will never experience again. The offer to move back to the USA in such a lucrative position and a role with a Fortune 10 company was a clear match and should have been easy to make. It checked off all the boxes for my career goals and ambitions. It would have positioned me very comfortably financially for the rest of my life. I turned down the offer. It was inexplicable except for that powerful force which overwhelmed the logic and rationale for taking the role.

Three things happened as a result, which I believe was this Divine intervention that forced me to turn down the role:

1. Two months later, our new Board of Directors informed my boss and me that they were not going to extend my contract (which was assumed to be a sure thing) even though I was turning 60 years old. In the UAE, the age of 60 is the retirement age for a government or semi-government company (which we were). The new Board wanted to stop the practice of making exceptions on extending executives beyond 60. I just turned down the most lucrative job in my life, and my contract was not being renewed.

2. About two weeks after being informed that I would have to retire a few months down the road when I turned 60, I got an unexpected call, completely out of the blue, from what is now my current company. This book sheds more light on this important period in my life.

3. Here is the most important bit: By not taking the AT&T role in Dallas, Texas, I ended up conceiving my only child, a son. My son was

born perfectly healthy in the Philippines. Under what still seem to be suspicious circumstances and questionable medical procedures, my son ended up with brain damage. According to the brain specialist from another hospital who conducted an MRI on his brain, the most plausible cause was due to lack of oxygen to the brain during seemingly dubious and perhaps unnecessary medical procedures and a series of surgeries. The MRI showed dead brain tissue (unrecoverable), and according to this doctor, a baby is not born with that condition. My son, Michael Todd, is the most pure and innocent child you could ever meet. As of this writing, he is nine years old. He will never be able to speak, still cannot eat food, only formula milk, and is still in diapers. He is my devotion in life and a pure blessing given to me by God. Was this the reason for the Divine intervention? To this day, I still believe there is a reason and purpose for my son living on this earth. All I know for now is that he is a precious gift with a pure and innocent heart who just wants to be loved and to love you right back. He is a pure blessing. He has blessed my life with such a deep and protective love and has given me a higher sense of purpose and devotion.

Now comes the part of the book that is special to me: Saudi Arabia. This is about my unexpected and most grateful experience, which has opened a whole new and amazing chapter in my life.

PART 3: SAUDI ARABIA

The People, Culture, and Values

2014 ---- 2024 (and ongoing as of this writing)

I was so apprehensive when I moved to Riyadh, Kingdom of Saudi Arabia. Though Dubai was my entrée into the Middle East, it was (and still is) my incredible and life-changing interactions with the people of Saudi Arabia where I experienced consistent, everyday kindness, welcoming, and acceptance. I did not expect this. It has been life-changing. I wish everyone, throughout their lives, or at least at some point in their lives, gets to experience what I have experienced. It reminds me of the Denzel Washington movie that came out in 2023, "Equalizer 3." The character, Robert McCall, played by Denzel Washington, falls in love with the people of this small Italian village and realizes he belongs there—all because of the way he is welcomed and treated and the ongoing and unexpected demonstrations of kindness. This is how I have felt every day in Saudi Arabia.

After my government-regulated retirement from my Vice President role in the UAE, I was offered a role at a highly recognized company in Riyadh. They allowed me to leverage my experience and take on an advisory role involving executive appointments, succession planning, talent development, coaching current and potential leaders, and managing a team of internal and external coaches. I continue in this capacity today (as of this writing). I also had an opportunity with another firm where I was an advisor to three Boards, a member of the executive committee, and led efforts to create a committee of the Board, the Human Capital & Compensation Committee, while acting as the Chief Talent & Leadership Development Officer.

Allow me to gladly share just a small sample of my everyday stories about the kindness, generosity, respect, and hospitality I have been privileged to experience. First, I think it is important to share a profound life lesson about the goodness of Islam and its compatibility with Christianity. Muslims respect Christianity. I believe that Muslims are more Christian than many Christians (which I will explain). I never would have learned these lessons if I had continued to live in the United States.

God (Allah) as the Foundation of Life

In Saudi Arabia, and with all Muslims, their lives start with their faith in God as the foundation. Saudis, and all Muslims, believe, and they truly believe, in God. One God. This is the first commandment of the Ten Commandments from Moses, i.e., One God. Christians are taught this, starting from the First Commandment from God to Moses. Moses, or Mousa, as the Muslims refer to him, is a recognized Prophet in Islam. Jesus even created the "Lord's Prayer," which starts, "Our Father, who art in Heaven, hallowed be thy name." Then, there is the Catholic prayer recited in church that begins with, "I believe in God, the Father Almighty, Creator of Heaven and earth, and all that is seen and unseen…."

The Muslim faith, as noted in the Quran, confirms what was written in the Jewish Torah, the Christian Gospels, as well as what was written by the Prophets before.

A Muslim Cannot Be a Muslim if They Do Not Believe in Jesus (Essa)

A Muslim cannot be a Muslim if they do not believe in Jesus (Essa). This surprises many Americans I speak with. Muslims revere Jesus (they refer to Him as "Essa"). Whenever they say the name of Jesus (Essa), they immediately say, "May peace be upon him." This is exactly what they say when they mention the name of their Prophet, Muhammed. They say, "May peace be upon him." They believe it is Jesus who will return, not the Prophet Muhammed. They believe Jesus was a great man, a

Prophet, and was born of the Virgin Mary. Jesus is mentioned throughout the entire Quran. They have stories about some of the miracles of Jesus, especially as a baby, that Christians have never heard of. They believe Jesus was a Prophet and not God, nor the Son of God. From my readings in the New Testament, the Christian Bible, Jesus never referred to himself as God. He always prayed to God as the "Father." He reinforced the First Commandment from Moses—One God.

Muslims do not pray to Muhammed. They pray to God, The One God. Since God plays a foundational role in the lives of Saudis, you will see no divisiveness, deep respect for each other, love of family, and clear adherence to their teachings. There is no controversy over what constitutes a man or woman. In fact, they believe in Adam and Eve and that Adam was a Prophet, as were Noah, Abraham, Isaac, Jacob, David, Moses, Jesus,

Muhammed, and others. They believe Muhammed (PBUH) was the last prophet from God (Allah).

The teachings of Islam and the Quran are an extension of Christianity. If you read the life story and history of the Prophet Muhammed (peace be upon him), who was born about 500 years after the death of Jesus, you will learn about a kind, forgiving, and most humble man who reinforced and lived the teachings of Jesus and all the Prophets and expanded upon those teachings as noted in the Quran.

The Holy Quran instructs Muslims to speak kindly and with respect to Christians and all faiths (Surah 5:82, Surah 2:62, Surah 5:69, Surah 61:14, etc.). Christians are respected and honored in Islam for their belief in God and their following of the Holy Scriptures. Christians are considered "people of the book." The Quran encourages dialogue and exchange of ideas with Christians in a just and compassionate manner. Muslims are taught to speak kindly to Christians, for they are the closest to you in faith. The Quran states: "and nearest among them in love to the believers will you find those who say, 'We are Christians,' because amongst these are men devoted to learning and men who are not arrogant." The Quran also says, "O, you who believe! Be helpers of God—as Jesus, the son of Mary, said to the disciples, 'Who will be my helpers in the work of God?'"

Belief in Mary (Miriam) and the Immaculate Conception

Like Christians, Muslims strongly believe in Mary (Maryam) and the Immaculate Conception. There is an entire chapter in the Quran devoted to Mary (she is referred to as Maryam, which is a very common female name in Islam). Not just Mary, but her family and her parents are described in the Quran. Mary is the only woman in the Quran mentioned by name. Not even the wives of the Prophet Muhammed are mentioned by name. They believe in Mary and honor her esteemed position among all women so strongly and in an unfettered and unified manner. Muslims believe all this, including the miracle of the Immaculate Conception, even more so than the general Christian population in countries that are becoming more secular. A phrase from the Quran says about Mary, "O Mary, Indeed Allah has chosen you and purified you and chosen you above the women of the worlds." The well-known Christian prayer says about Mary, "Hail Mary, full of grace, blessed art thou among women...."

Belief in the Angels

The Muslim faith is consistent with Christianity in its belief in angels, starting with the most prominent archangels, Gabriel (referred to as Jibril) and Michael (Mikail). It was Gabriel who recited the Quran directly to the Prophet Muhammed, who was illiterate yet still able to recite, word-for-word, the message from God through the Angel Gabriel. It was Gabriel who also announced the coming of Jesus to John the Baptist.

A Few Samples of the Practical Teachings (Hadith) of the Muslim Faith

A colleague once gave me a book called "200 Hadith." This book is approved by the Presidency of Islamic Research, Ifta and Propagation (Riyadh, Saudi Arabia), the Ministry of Information (Makkah, Saudi Arabia), and the Muslim World League (Makkah, Saudi Arabia). Hadith means "the sayings and doings of the Prophet Muhammed" (peace be upon him). From reading the book, I found that the teachings were all about being a good human being every single day. The Hadith addresses many aspects of life, such as manners, war and peace, trade, the pursuit of knowledge, health, family rights, parents' rights, marriage and divorce, being charitable, debts, and more. I wish I could share many more of the teachings, but here are a few samples of what I discovered:

- **Killing an Innocent Person**: "If anyone killed a person not in retaliation of murder or to spread mischief in the land, it would be as if he killed all mankind, and if anyone saved a life, it would be as if he saved the life of all mankind." (Quran, Surah 5, Verse 32). Muslims in the Middle East are some of the most peaceful and kindest people I have met in my lifetime. They are not terrorists. In fact, they abhor terrorism, and if and when they find a terrorist cell, trust me, that cell and those terrorists are dealt with swiftly and severely. We just don't hear about it. Muslims in the Middle East are the most family-oriented, welcoming, and kindest people I have ever met. I have always felt enormously safe to walk anywhere or be anywhere. The USA is a Christian country, and the Ku Klux Klan was a Christian-based organization, and the institution of slavery took place in the southern part of a Christian country, yet those practices certainly do not represent the teachings of Christianity.

- **Charity and Good Deeds**: According to the Hadith, "every good deed is a charity." Saying a good word is charity, picking up litter off the street is charity, acting justly between two people is charity, helping others is charity, meeting someone with a cheerful face is charity, etc. And it goes on. Of course, donating within your means to those people or families in need is considered charity, and it is one of the Five Pillars of Islam, called Zakat. The Hadith says, "Every part of a person's body must perform a charity every day the sun comes up; to act justly between two people is a charity; to help a man with his mount, lifting him onto it or hoisting his belongings onto it is a charity; a good word is a charity; every step you take to prayers is a charity; and removing a harmful thing from the road is a charity. Do not consider even the smallest good deed as insignificant—even meeting your brother with a smile is a charity." "Allah does not judge according to your bodies and appearances, but He scans your hearts and looks into your deeds." The Hadith also says, "You should show courtesy and be cordial with each other, so that nobody should consider himself superior to another or harm him." I see pure cordiality every day with the Saudi people, as they are so cordial to me on an everyday basis. There are other Hadith around manners and good deeds as they relate to envy, talking behind someone's back, and the qualities of "mildness" and "toleration." The list goes on. These are the practices and behaviors I see every day.

- **Good Manners**: The Hadith says, "Virtue is good conduct," and virtue refers to any good deed. "Allah likes kindness in all things." "To feed people and to greet everyone (to say Assalam Alaikum) whether you know him or not." The greeting of "Assalam Alaikum" means "peace be upon you." Being humble and not showing superiority is good manners. Talking about someone behind their back and being envious or jealous is not accepted. I have been privileged to have dinners at people's homes, and I love when I see everyone go to the eldest and kiss their forehead out of love and respect. It is beautiful to see. I see it when younger brothers kiss their older brother on the forehead. The Hadith says, "A younger person should greet an elder one." I see this all the time, and it is a beautiful part of their culture. The teachings say that "God scans one's heart and looks into one's deeds." The common greeting of "Assalam Alaikum" (peace be upon you) when greeting someone is considered a good deed and good manners.

- **Family and Relatives—and Women and Wives Treated Very Well**: The teaching from their Prophet states, "The most perfect man in his faith among the believers is the one with the best character among them, and the best of you are those who are best to their wives." This is so true regardless of what we hear in the media. Women and wives are treated with respect per their teachings. I see how women are treated with great respect every single day where I work. Something as simple as a full elevator and a woman wants to get on, and a man will get off the elevator so the woman can get on. Disobedience to parents is unacceptable (this is also one of the Ten Commandments from Moses, which states, "Honor Thy Mother and Father"). Mothers and fathers are truly honored in Arab society. This Hadith teaches that it is

45

unacceptable for anyone to break off relations with his family by not visiting them or helping them—"He who breaks off ties of blood will not enter paradise." This is why I consistently see a family bond. More about parents, "Allah (God) forbids all of you to disobey your mothers." Speaking of mothers, the Hadith also teaches that the most important person in the family is the mother, the second most important is the mother, and the third most important is the mother... then the father. The Hadith says, "A man asked the Messenger of Allah (peace be upon him), 'Who amongst his near ones had the greatest right over him?'" The Prophet replied, "Your mother." He again asked, "Then who is next?" The Prophet replied, "Your mother." He asked again, "Then who is next?" The Prophet replied, "Your mother." He asked, "Then who is next?" The Prophet replied, "Your father."

- **Kindness to Animals**: Even kindness to animals, such as giving a hungry or thirsty cat or dog food and water, is viewed positively by God (Allah). As noted in the Hadith, "A woman was tormented because of a cat which she had confined and starved until it died. She did not allow it to eat or drink while it was confined, nor did she free it so that it might eat the insects of the earth. As a result of her evilness, she was condemned to Hell." "A man walking along a path felt very thirsty. Reaching a well, he descended into it, drank water to his fill, and came out. Then he saw a dog with its tongue hanging out, trying to lick up mud to quench its thirst. The man said to himself that the dog was feeling the same extreme thirst as he had felt a little while ago. So he descended once more into the well, filled his leather hosier with water, came up holding it by his teeth, and gave the dog a drink. Allah appreciated the act of this man and forgave his sins." It goes on to say, "There is re-compensation for kindness to every living thing."

OTHER TRUTHS and OBSERVATIONS

Women Are Treated Very Well

For non-Muslims and many Westerners, here is a surprise: women are treated with great respect and certainly love from their families. Saudi women are so proud of their country, their culture, and their faith. They are treated with the utmost respect. This is completely contrary to the perception created, in large part, by the media. I am speaking from factual, first-hand experience and observations. All you have to do is ask any Saudi woman. They wear abayas because they want to. In fact, you should see the incredible, beautiful styles and colors of abayas today. It is about fashion now. If they cover their face, it is because of a family or personal decision. Their religion does not require women to cover their face. As noted earlier, the teachings of Islam state that men must treat their wives with respect and that the three most important people in the family are: 1) The Mother, 2) The Mother, 3) The Mother. Then, the father is next.

Saudi Arabia is opening up the corporate and professional world to women. I work with a few thousand Saudi women and am amazed at their intelligence, career goals, ambition, drive for achievement, humility, strength, and wonderful sense of humor. Many in my company are categorized as "High-Potential Leaders." To see them demonstrate their executive presence and present with confidence, substance, and insight is impressive.

On a personal note, one of my roles is Executive Appointments. This means I come in during the final stage of appointing someone for promotion to

General Manager or Vice President. Of course, we try to promote internally first, but sometimes we hire from the outside. I played a pivotal role in recommending for hire the first female executive in our company. Since then, I was asked to coach her for a next-level promotion. I have also played a role in recommending other talented women for General Manager roles. These appointments were well-deserved and with merit. Since I work with so many Saudi women, I have come to realize they are like women in every part of the world and possess a great sense of humor. They are amazing daughters, wives, and mothers, and they cherish those roles deeply as part of their faith and upbringing.

The Significance of the Family and Honoring the Parents and Elders

One of the Ten Commandments from Moses in the Bible is "Honor Thy Mother and Father." Saudis honor their parents throughout their lives. The love and respect given to mothers and fathers up until they leave this earth is a profound thing to observe. Their teachings (Hadith) and values are consistent with the Ten Commandments. Parents are taken care of by their adult sons and daughters. I know a number of senior executives in my company who make it a practice to either call their mothers or parents every night or stop by to see them before going home to their wife and children. The family is everything, and it is against their teachings to break away from the family. Even younger brothers will kiss their older brothers on the forehead. When I have had dinners at home, I see all the men line up to kiss the eldest man (usually the grandfather) on the forehead out of love and respect. The family bond begins with honoring their mother and father.

The Beauty of Ramadan

Ramadan is one of the five pillars of Islam, and it is a special time of year for all Muslims. It is a time of fasting from eating or drinking (from dawn until dusk) even while working. It is a time of prayer, reflection, and contemplating one's relationship with God (Allah), a time of empathy, sacrifice, and self-discipline. It is a time that encourages one to be mindful of the blessings in our lives and mindful of those less fortunate, which manifests in increased generosity, charity, and a sense of community. What makes Ramadan so special for Muslims is the bonding of family, friends, and neighbors. It is amazing to see. I have been invited to a number of homes to break the fast in the early evening, and the food is often greater than the Thanksgiving meals I have experienced over the years in the United States. The difference is that this happens every night for the month of Ramadan. Ramadan reinforces the love of family, the greater family, friends, and neighbors. It is a very special time and the most holy time of the year for all Saudi citizens and Muslims around the world. It is beautiful to see the love and bonding of family and community while reflecting on their relationship with God and each other.

The Kingdom Form of Government

Allow me to share my views, observations, and experiences about the Kingdom form of government. Here is what I see very clearly. Having grown up in a democracy, I was suspicious all my life that any other form of government was not quite as good. I have since learned that there are other good forms of government. Since the modern Kingdom of Saudi Arabia was founded in 1932 by King Abdulaziz Al Saud, the succession of the Kingdom has gone to each of his sons. Each King, from King Saud, King Faisal, King Khalid, King Fahd, King Abdullah, and the current King Salman (with the Crown Prince Mohammed bin Salman, affectionately referred to as "MBS"), has been altruistic by looking out for the greater good of the country and its citizens. The Saudi citizens love their form of government. There is no divisiveness. There is almost complete unity. One will not see protests where buildings are burned down and looting occurs inside small or major retailers. Saudis are proud of their country, their culture, their families, their King, and their God. The Saudi citizens are treated very well. They have no interest whatsoever in experiencing a democratic form of government. During Covid, the government did amazing things to ensure not only their own citizens but even expats like myself were taken care of with the original vaccinations and the booster shots that followed. Back to the democracy form of government, which is an admirable form of government when it is applied according to the intent. But when mean-spirited intentions and behaviors abound quite frequently, when federal enforcement is weaponized against those with differing views, or when the precious First Amendment guaranteeing free speech is in jeopardy, there are perilous risks. I remember a quote by Winston Churchill, who said, "If you want to build a case against democracy, just talk to the average voter for five minutes." Saudis love their unity and the altruistic history of their Kings. It is perfect timing for their Vision 2030.

Saudi Vision 2030

In 2015, the Kingdom of Saudi Arabia announced an ambitious Vision to be realized by 2030. The results have been transformative—a word often overused in business but not in the case of this Saudi vision. The Vision focuses on three main pillars: "A thriving economy, a vibrant society, and an ambitious nation." Like many visions that sound idealistic on paper, I was skeptical. It was 15 years away, and I have learned over the years that it is not what the vision says but what the vision does. An amazing publicity campaign ensued, and today, as of this writing in 2024, it seems that all Saudi citizens are familiar to varying degrees with the country's Vision 2030. The Saudi citizens are all unified, and there is no evidence of divisiveness. What is amazing is that the vision has been happening and continues to happen. Digital transformation is in clear view to enable a thriving economy, an ambitious nation, and a vibrant society. Why is this vision actually being realized and moving forward in such an impressive fashion? I believe it is because of the ambitions and talent of Saudis, as well as the strong leadership of their Crown Prince (Mohammed Bin Salman or "MBS"), along with a determined and focused implementation process that has led to incredible progress. The Saudi Public Investment Fund (PIF) has funded many new companies to grow the economy and the prosperity of the country far beyond the gas and oil industry. Gas and oil have been the mainstay of the Saudi economy for years, but a country cannot depend on just one dominant industry to sustain its future growth. Many diversified companies and industries are in play now. Saudi Arabia is in the lead globally towards becoming a digitally enabled economy. Saudi Arabia is flying with great momentum, and the Saudi citizens could not be more united and proud.

Watch out for Saudi Arabia. The cultural and societal changes since 2015 have been precipitous, and the changes continue to happen in an amazing fashion. The economic changes and the growth of new industries and companies are keeping up with the cultural and societal changes. I have been experiencing a first-hand view of the transformation of Saudi Arabia, and again, the citizens are very proud.

Saudi Talent and Work Ethic: They Are Second-to-None

In my role, I work very closely with leadership talent from senior executives to entry-level college graduates. I put Saudi professional talent second to none. By the way, I am including women as well. Much of the world thinks Saudi Arabia mistreats their women. As I mentioned earlier, this is far from the truth. We have a high percentage of females selected and categorized as "high-potentials." They are as ambitious, engaged, and committed to their work and careers as the men are. I have coached and continue to coach many of the men and women at all levels (executive to recent graduates), so I am convinced of the talent and future potential. They are ambitious and want to experience success no differently than anyone else. They are willing to work hard, drive for results, develop and grow themselves into leadership or expert roles, and make a contribution not just to their company but to their country. This is very evident to me on an everyday basis. I worked closely with hundreds of McKinsey consultants years ago as a coach. McKinsey is arguably the most prestigious management consulting firm in the world. They hire from the top universities around the world and those with outstanding academic achievement. They also hire young talent willing to work hard to develop and grow. I put the young professionals and the experienced leaders in my company and other Saudi companies second to none, including McKinsey. The energy, motivation, and drive, the willingness to work hard and develop their knowledge and capabilities is clearly evident to me. So impressive. The future is bright for Saudi and its citizens.

Health Care

As an American expat working in Saudi Arabia, I do not pay a single penny (or Saudi Riyal) for health care. Health care is provided to all employees and, in many cases, even to their parents! In 2016, I was hospitalized for 12 days for a ruptured appendix. I was in Boston when it ruptured but did not realize it was ruptured. I boarded my flight that evening from Boston to Dubai to Riyadh with a ruptured appendix. The doctors could not figure out how I dealt with the pain, but they had a theory. The rupture caused poison and even gangrene, and they felt it cushioned the pain. The doctors told me I was lucky to survive without septic shock occurring or other associated complications from this event. During the 12 days, I had a drain into my stomach that drained all the poison and antibiotic. The medical care was amazing. After 12 days, my total out-of-pocket expense was 100 Saudi Riyals (about $30 U.S.). During Covid, we were all covered by the government without touching our medical insurance. The Saudi government paid for everyone's (expats included) Covid vaccines and booster shots.

Working for a Member of the Royal Family

I am sensitive about this section because I want to protect the privacy of a former boss of mine, a member of the Saudi Royal Family. He is a Royal Highness Prince, a Harvard MBA, brilliant, with a great sense of humor, and a very humble man. He is a descendant of two Kings (one from his mother's side and one from his father's side). He told me one day about the first car his grandfather (a former King) bought him. I was expecting to hear about a high-end brand. I laughed when he told me it was an old used Buick with an ugly brown color. That shows the values he was raised on and the values the King, his grandfather, wished to convey to him. This gentleman was the President of the family business. I was assigned to a number of executive and board advisory roles for this company. One light story here: I was attending a board meeting (my advisory role) with one of the subsidiary boards. This subsidiary owned a large number of popular and well-managed restaurants. The board decided to have lunch in one of the newly opened restaurants. I ended up in the car with His Royal Highness driving. We arrived at the restaurant, and all of the staff were waiting with excitement to meet His Royal Highness. We walked into the restaurant with the staff all lined up to greet him. I was right behind, shaking everyone's hand, and they had no idea who I was except that I accompanied His Royal Highness. You could say this was my 15 minutes of fame (or more like 3 minutes).

When I contacted His Royal Highness during the writing of this book, I told him my draft included a small segment about him. I sought his permission and offered if he wanted to review what I wrote. His kindness and humility were on display when he said, "It's okay, Mike. I don't need to review it. I trust you, and good luck with the book."

Generosity and Hospitality

This is where I have accumulated many stories. I am so grateful and honored to have been invited to people's homes for lunches or dinners. In the United States, in November, we have one of our most popular holidays – Thanksgiving. It is a day when the average guest like me eats so much food we can barely walk afterward. Being a guest in a Saudi home, it is double or triple the amount of food. The hosts are not satisfied if you only have one serving. They want you to have at least three servings! Even if one says "no thank you" to a second or third serving, they will still put more food on your plate whether you want it or not (I often laugh when telling these stories). Saudis just want to treat you as a VIP guest. It is in their culture, their values, and their way of life. I treasure these memories, and I am forever grateful for being treated with such hospitality.

One day, I was in a meeting. A colleague (and friend) of mine, a General Manager, walked by me, and I happened to say, "Fahd, I love the cologne! What is the brand?" He told me, "It's Prada." The next day, I was in my office, and I got a call from Fahd's secretary. The secretary said, "Mike, Fahd would like you to come to his office. He has something for you." I walked to his office, and there was a beautifully wrapped gift, and inside was a bottle of the Prada cologne. I learned my lesson NOT to compliment anyone on their cologne, or a nice pen (yes, one guy tried to force me to take his very expensive Mont Blanc pen, which I innocently complimented). I won that battle by telling him that I love the Saudi culture of generosity but please respect my culture to compliment when I see something to compliment. It is the guidance and teaching of Prophet Muhammad (peace be upon him): "You will not be considered a faithful person till you perform generosity to your guest." Today, I am very careful about giving a compliment on a product someone personally owns.

Finally, allow me to go back to the days when I first traveled to Dubai and Abu Dhabi back in early 1996. I was facilitating a session with the top 100 executives, starting with the top 20. Just about everyone came up and invited me to spend one of the weekend days with them so they could show me around their country, the United Arab Emirates. I accepted the offer from the first executive who invited me. He spent his entire day off driving me through five of the seven Emirates. An amazing day. Just another gesture of kindness and hospitality that the culture takes for granted and a gesture I will always remember, including the executive's name (Yahyah).

Feeling Welcomed and Treated with Kindness

There is a lot of talk around the world about "diversity and inclusion." Yet, the Middle East, and my company included, values diversity and believes that diversity for diversity's sake is incomplete if it does not coincide and align with making everyone feel included. Here is my bottom-from-my-heart experience:

One final story about being welcomed and feeling valued by the people of Saudi: Unlike my home country, which gave me a good start in my work career and provided me with immeasurable education for which I will always be grateful, Saudi Arabia and the Middle East did not care that I was in my 60s. What they cared about was 1) the quality of the relationship and 2) trust in my ability to contribute value to the organization. The end result is that they made a special accommodation to allow me to continue working and contributing until the age of 70. This is one of the highest compliments and displays of appreciation I have ever experienced in my life.

How About a Balanced View: Are There Areas that are Not So Positive?

Okay, I realize that everything you have read so far sounds so positive about Saudi Arabia and the Middle East. I should balance this book with areas of improvement. The first for me is the crazy driving and the constant beeping of horns. I say this with a little lightness and a smile, but it's true. One of my first decisions when I moved to Riyadh, Saudi Arabia, was not to lease a car and drive but to find a personal driver. I drove my own car in Dubai and Abu Dhabi but not in Saudi Arabia. I can't tell you how many times I've had to have a serious discussion with an Uber driver making me feel unsafe. I have witnessed many accidents, not serious accidents, but small accidents almost every day causing traffic delays. The interesting part is that when an accident happens, the cars must stay where they are; they must not pull over to the side of the road. They must wait for the insurance company to arrive and investigate first-hand. The other interesting thing is that both sides in the accident are kind and respectful to each other.

As an American, I am not used to cars always beeping their horns. Americans don't beep their horns unless it is a last resort necessity. Drivers in other parts of the world, including the Middle East, tend to beep their horns a lot. It seems the drivers find many reasons to beep their horns. If you are stopped at a traffic light and the light turns green, you can count on numerous cars far behind you honking their horns. So, I am still getting used to the liberal use of drivers beeping their horns. In the United States, it is commonly known that the pedestrian has the right of way, especially in a crosswalk. Not so in other countries. Many drivers will not stop for a pedestrian crossing the street, even if in the crosswalk.

FINAL THOUGHTS – MY LIFE ENHANCED

I love visiting my hometown roots outside of Boston and my home in New Hampshire. I love visiting the ocean coast of Massachusetts, Maine, Cape Cod, and the islands of Nantucket and Martha's Vineyard. I love going back to experience the mountains and lakes of New Hampshire and the countryside of Vermont. But I am eternally grateful for feeling consistently welcomed with kindness and respect on an everyday basis by my dear friends, colleagues, and all the citizens of Saudi Arabia I have come across. I wish every person on this planet could experience the type of welcoming and kindness I have received. Living in Saudi Arabia has been an unexpectedly amazing journey, and I am eternally grateful. I have learned how important it is to live in a country where the greatest and strongest foundation in their lives is God (Allah). The unity, lack of divisiveness, the values and teachings of their Hadith and their Prophet

Muhammed (may peace be upon him), and their belief in Jesus (may peace be upon him) give me unequivocal confidence that Saudi Arabia will achieve their Vision 2030 and beyond and become a major global economic force. In fact, their vision is already underway. It is already happening. We don't have to wait until 2030. We can all learn from the values and culture of Saudi Arabia, just as they continue to learn about what made America great. They love the United States of America. They are pained and confused by what they see (the decline of values and a seeming increase in secularism, which is causing a much too strong divide). I continue to have hope and deep and abiding love for my home country. I also have hope, confidence, and best wishes for Saudi Arabia to continue to thrive while maintaining their values of family (honoring the parents and the role of the mother as the first, second, and third most important person in the family, and that the best of men are those who treat their wives well), while demonstrating good manners, charity, and good deeds. I wish my friends peace with each other, with God as their foundation and compass in life.